Book of
Poetry

WORDS OF ENCOURAGEMENT

FLORENCE PETERSON

ISBN 978-1-0980-7229-2 (paperback)
ISBN 978-1-0980-7230-8 (digital)

Christian Faith Publishing, Inc.
832 Park Avenue
Meadville, PA 16335
www.christianfaithpublishing.com

Printed in the United States of America

The Rain

Each time a child is beaten
Or, through injustice
A man's life is claimed

When things seem, so empty
And no hope seems to remain
When promises, are broken
And hatred, turns into pain

Here comes, his tears from *heaven*
Its name is called, the rain

Our Lord knows all, the answers
To us, he makes it plain

Here comes, his tears from *heaven*
Its name is called, the rain

We live in a world, that's shaken
Whose name, is called insane
But, look up toward, the *heavens*
Because, God calls it, his rain

Receive the Lord

I cannot fight your battles
It's not for me, to do.

The battles, that you're having
Are with God, and only you.

In your trials, and tribulations
Your spirit, was broken today
But seek, your comfort in
God's love, his light, and his way.

So be strong with peace he gives us
It's all, a part of his plans.

The final answers
Are in God's hands
And will never, be
Those of a man's.

Believe

Trust with your heart,
Renew with your mind.
So peace, hope, and joy,
You can easily find.
All these things come,
To those that believe.
Take time to find them,
So your dreams can be retrieved.

God's Way

Hope to cope
Live to give
Love from Above
Not less, but more bless
No fears, less tears
God's plans, for man

Humbly Believe

Humbly ask
Faithfully believe
Pray for your answers
So your heart,
Won't be grieved.

Until I'm Gray
And Old

It's not about the riches
It's not about the gold
It's about living
In God's words
Until I'm gray and old.

There's Something I Need to Change

There's something I need
To place
Here within my plans
God, is always on
The throne
And the devil
Is just a man

His Gifts

Lord, you are my soul, my spirit
A song, in my heart, you bring.

Today, I pause to thank you
For each, and everything.

Another day, you've given me.
Helping me to continue
To strive and to cope.
What a gift, a *shining light*
That gives me, so much hope.

Lord, you have always stayed beside me
Here, you have always been.

Thank you for being my
Lord and Savior.
And now, for becoming
My friend.

Peace to Fullness

A peaceful heart
A cold wet rain
A snow-capped mountain
Sitting high on the plain.

A gentle breeze, blowing quickly by
A dream that comes true
And reaches, high in the skies.

A child who has a beautiful smile
To walk for a, long, and winding mile.

A hand that reaches down when one falls
To listen intensely, as your name is being called.

The opening of, my eyes to see
All the plans you have set before me.

Family Ties

Family ties are, so sacred today
As each go, their separate ways.

No time to reach, for that open door
Roots that are grown from their
Deepest core.

Strong Family ties, which
Link us, as one
A mother, a father
Daughters, and sons.

I thank you Lord
This is what a family
Is about.

Love, joy, and peace
And no self-doubt.

A planted seed that you
Help grow
All by connecting us
From head to toe.

I Pray Don't Let Me Go Astray

Lord, keep me in Remembrance
Don't let me go astray.
I know my Jesus loves me
Each and every day.

When worries try to approach me
And I cannot find my way,
I know my Jesus loves me
Each and every day.

When sorrows can burn so deeply
And pain won't go away,
I know my Jesus loves me
Each and every day.

My heart is filled with gladness
And joy on this very day.
I've asked the Lord to keep me
And don't let me go astray.

Lord, you always keep your promises
And so on this very day.
I'll continue living through your words
And will always continue to pray.

The Answers

When troubles try to find you
And your pain won't go away.
It's Jesus that has the answers
Not yesterday but today.
When life that you're living
Brings you down on your knees to pray
Know it's Jesus that has the answers
Not yesterday but today.
In his comforting arms
You will find
Our Savior all the time.
Yes, it's Jesus that has the answers
Not yesterday but today.

Joyful Blessings

Lord I can feel how you are
Shaping me and as you mold.

This *ungodly* heart
That is so very cold.

Here, awaiting to see.
The glory of your face,
Blessed by your mercies
And your tender grace.

Continue to help me,
To do what, I must do.
I'll keep enjoying
The peace and your joy,
Which can only be received
Through you.

Redeemed and Renewed

He has taken away my, cancer
He has taken away my, stroke
Relieved me from my, hardships
Removed me from this yoke.

He heals, he fixes, and yes he
Also mold
He is my rock, my strength
Who lives within my soul.

Happiness is my agenda.
Pain has gone, down below.
His peace, he placed within my heart,
I will worship, so I can grow.

I will lift my hands toward
your heavens
Your blessings, you do unfold
All the stories, of my past
Has become so very old.

I will raise, my hands
Toward *your heavens*
Because Jesus you are my goal.

It's time to have a new life,
A new Hope,
And a brand-new role.

Words of Encouragement

Love can turn, an angry man around,
But, with hatred, in his heart,
Love will never be found.

Tears comes with, heartaches, and pain,
But, a good laughter, will correct,
A heart that is vain.

It's not for us
To correct.
We are, to give it
To God
And he'll redirect.

Be humble.
Be grateful.
Be kind.

Faith is where
The heart and soul meet.
So, that the spirit
Can be free.

God is good, God is great
He knows, my heart
He knows, my fate.

The Lord's love
Have anchored, my heart
And has built up my soul.

Lord, open my eyes
So, I can see
All your plans
You set before me.

Lord, keep me in your sight
Continue to let me do
What's right.
And strengthen me
With all your might.

Let your past
Be forgotten
And your
Future be enjoyed.

One man's mistake
Is another man's
Correction.

Selfishness, starts when
We walk away from
God's plans
Because we think
Ours are better.

When one says, "I will"
It is not the same as
"It is done."

A person can have many friends
But, it's better to be a *friend*.

Call on the Lord
He's waiting
To give you
Your answers.

Lonely people
Are people
Who have not
Searched for God yet.

No matter how much
The devil *taunt me*
And try to put me
In chains
I know my Lord
Will save me
In him I shall remain.

Peace calms the soul
And being courageous
Can make one strong.

But, a man who believes
It's hard to pray
His fall, won't be
Very long.

A peaceful heart
A soul that is tamed
A body controlled
Gives joy, a new name.

Two hands are good
But four hands
Are better

You can't see
If you keep getting
blindsided

The littlest things
Make the biggest
Differences
As long as it
Can be heard

Time don't count
If you waste it
Incorrectly

All things go through
The hands of God
He is the judge of *all*

God is my rock
My heart and my soul
He shapes, he fixes
And, he can also
MOLD

The root of every family
Is the branches
That grows
From its trees

All of our answers are
From God, who's above
Sprinkled with his grace
And all of his love

Peace can control
All of one's mind
But, an unruly person
Will get left behind

What man can control
All of his life?
When he can't even control
That unruly wife

If you truly want
To be blessed
Follow God's plans
And he'll do the rest

Lord, help me to get rid of
Self-centeredness
And self-righteousness

But, help me to find
Self-control
So, I can focus only on you

Lord, help set me free
Not only, from all my
Troubles
But, this woman, I call me

Ask the Lord
For what you need
Remember, your mind
He can already read

A peaceful soul, will
Quiet the noise

You can't hear
If you are
Talking
By the time we complain
It's over

I will keep peace
In my heart
For God is the kingdom
The Holy Spirit, is my guidance
And Jesus is my Savior

In order to teach
One must
First be taught

An open heart
Produces
A welcoming hand

Keep feeding the SOUL

Forgiveness Prayer

Dear family and friends,
Today on this day, I ask
If I have offended, or
Hurt you, in any way,
May God place a blessing
On these words,
Forgive Me.
My hope is that, you receive
Them in love; may we all
Have a blessed-filled day,
And be thankful, thoughtful,
And kind, toward each other.

In Jesus' name. Amen.

God's Gift

Each day, is a gift
God gives to, me and you.
Telling us the things, he wants us to do.

Sending us his *Peace*, happiness, and his joy
Received by, each little girls, and boys.
Expressing his love, especially for you.
Reminding us, his love, is gracious and so true.

Love

Search out, the answer.
Why should we love others?
The answer is so easy.
God says, "Love one another."

You brothers, and sisters
Your daughters, and sons
Our mothers, and fathers
All joined in, as one.

What's so hard about giving up
This thing we call "Our Love"
When we receive it so freely,
From our Father, who's above.

Today, take time, to show
Someone you care.

Then also, let it be known
That you will always,
Be there.

He Can

Our Lord, can take away
Your troubles.
He can cover up your pain.

He can clean up your anger
And make you, wanting to change.

He can make your days so much better.
And work on, all your plans.

Not asking us, for anything
'Cause it all comes, through his Hands.

When your troubles, catch up with you
While you're walking on your way,

Just know it's never too late
To get on, your knees and pray.

Greatness

All of your mountains, and all of your plains
You look down upon us, as you sit and do reign

Your awesomeness, your beauty, your greatness
Forever remains

Your sun, your moon, your stars
All forever *unexplained*

Oh! Let us rejoice, in your presence
We are truly blessed

To be in your comforting Arms
And partakers of your *Rest*

It Is the Jesus in You

No matter how many roads
I travelled

No matter how many things
I do

The road that I'm going ON
My, Lord, it leads to you

Each day we receive your blessings
So perfect in every way

Another gift you given us
Your faithfulness do show
May our hearts, mind, and souls
Continue to grow and grow

To Care

To care—means to always be there
And knowing that, we're willing to share.

Also choosing ways, to be FAIR
It can also mean to help, and to bear
And no it's not, so very rare
It only requires, that we be somewhere
If not in a group, at least as pair
So today I want, to give you a dare
Go out and tell somebody
That you do CARE.

Why?

Why do we worry?
Why do we cry?
Why do we think
In this life, we'll get by?

Why do we argue?
Why do we fight?
Why not, search for Jesus?
Our strength, and our might?

Why do we hurt others?
Why do we demand?
Why can't we realize
That our Master, really can?

Why do we hurt, the ones we love?
When all of our answers
Comes from our Savior, who's above.

So let's get rid of all of these *Whys*
Because we know, who's in control
Over all of our lives.

His Hands

Are you living from,
The beauty, inside of you?
Are you listening, to what
God's telling you to do?

Or, are you living
On your own plans?
Seeking answers, but
Finding demands?

Are you travelling, on
A road that's holding
You back?

Is love, that something,
You always lack?

Now is the time to
Turn to God's plans.
He'll welcome you, with love
And, the opening, of his hands.

Jesus Can

I know of a man
Named Jesus
Who one day, taken me
By the hand
He said, If you will listen
I'll tell you all my plans

Your heart, you've already
Given me
It's placed safely
Within my hands
But your soul is also required
For it, too, is part of a man

Your body, is my temple
Let's try to keep it right
I've covered, all your battles
No longer you need to fight

So be blessed, my little children
Just keep doing my commands
Never think, there's nothing
I can't do
Haven't I've shown you
Jesus Can

Peace

Peace, is that friend
Who never wants to let go

It seeks to strengthen you
As you continue, to grow

It's the kind of warmth,
That's hard to explain

Never wanting to leave,
Holding on, to remain

It's that feeling that you have
In someone, you can trust

It's not just a need,
It becomes a part of us

And when you catch it,
Never let it part

It's the most beautiful thing
That comes, from your heart.

Worrying for (Naught) "Nothing"

It's God, who can
Change a man's heart

So yes, all my worries
Have been for nought

All of my battles
Are won, that he fought
So yes, all my worries
Has been for nought

All of my enemies
Whom my demise, they sought
God revealed them to me
And my worries were
For nought

The things, I have learnt
And what, I have been taught

To stop worrying
'Cause, it's all done
For nought.

Words of Encouragement

The outside of a man,
Is his covering
But the inside of a man,
Is God's *hovering*

Let's try to be of
Few words,
So that during that
Quietness,
Others can be heard

Keep Your Humbleness Before You

I remember that, trying day
So lost, that I could not find my way
Blind I was, that I could not see
Blessed I was because you came
And rescued me.

You counted each of my footsteps
That I would, have to make
You knew each breath, that I
Would have to take.

Continuing to provide for me
From day to day to day
Giving me your Hope and Strength
Then sent me on my way.

Keep Me

Lord, continue to keep me
Safe under your wing

Thankful I am, for the peace
That you bring

I will keep in remembrance
How you give me your love
Given by your grace
Which you send, from above

Lord keep me, running to you
When troubles come my way
Knowing that, you are
The planner, of all my days

Joyful

What a Joy! That the Lord
Gives us, all our plans
Which he keeps, securely
In His hands

Always placing us, close within
His heart
Never wanting us, to be so
Far apart

We are always in his presence
He helps us, see another day
Preventing us, from trying
To go astray

What a joyful blessing
To all of us he bring
Placing within our hearts
A beautiful song, to sing

I Just (Wanna) Thank You

I just wanna, thank you Lord
On this trying day
You opened up my eyes
To a much better *way*

You kept me safe, so we will never part
While pulling on, the stings of my heart

You've made this day, a very joyful one
Conquering my problems, so there is none
I thank you Lord for being so very kind
Giving me your day, and having it become mine

If I

If I can only do it
If I can

If the world, would show me
That life is not so bland

If people could love me
And they become my fans

If life didn't have so many demands

If I could tear up, all of my plans
And place all of my *ifs*
In the safety of Jesus's hands

Our Heart

Our heart is God's token
It truly is our gift

Each day, the Lord
Moves it and gives
It a lift

Trouble comes, a short time
For some

The more we focus on them
The bigger, they become
The Lord knows, all our troubles
Yes, he's fully aware
That's why he's always
Telling us,
To look up, because
He'll always be there

Time

A second, a minute, an hour a day.
This is how we should live.
Yes, that is the way.

We live in bitterness, anger, and strife.
Not only today, but most of our life.

Time will never be placed in our hands.
It's a part of God's *unknown* plans.
Our Father gives us the answers
As to what we must DO.
He is the *Master Planner*
Of all of it too.

Tomorrow

Tomorrow is not given
It's only in God's hands
It may be filled with hardships
And so many demands

So be careful what you wish for
It may only be *Your Plans*
Remember all our tomorrows
Come through *His Hands*

Let's pray for his strength
His courage and his might
Our stories are already completed
And have already been made right

Each day our hearts, he comforts
And he fills
Just asking us to follow him
And to try and do His Will.

About the Author

The author, Florence Peterson, is from a small city called Chester, Pennsylvania. She is a longtime writer of poems throughout her life-time. She is the sister of nine other siblings, all girls. She has a daugh-ter whose name is Danielle and two granddaughters whose names are Seoni and Taraji. She hopes you will enjoy reading this book.